COOL CAREERS WITHOUT COLLEGE
FOR PEOPLE WHO LOVE

WRITING AND
BLOGGING

REBECCA PELOS AND GREG ROZA

Rosen
YA
™

New York

Published in 2018 by The Rosen Publishing Group, Inc.
29 East 21st Street, New York, NY 10010

Copyright © 2018 by The Rosen Publishing Group, Inc.

First Edition

Library of Congress Cataloging-in-Publication Data

Names: Pelos, Rebecca, author. | Roza, Greg, author.
Title: Cool careers without college for people who love writing and blogging / Rebecca Pelos and Greg Roza.
Description: First edition. | New York, NY : Rosen Publishing, [2018] | Series: Cool careers without college | Includes bibliographical references and index.
Identifiers: ISBN 9781508175469 (library bound)
Subjects: LCSH: Authorship—Vocational guidance—Juvenile literature. | Writing services—Vocational guidance—Juvenile literature. | Blogs—Vocational guidance—Juvenile literature.
Classification: LCC PN159.P45 2018 | DDC 808.02—dc23

Manufactured in China

CONTENTS

INTRODUCTION

When you think of a writer, your vision is often of a famous novelist at a book signing or typing away on his or her latest novel in the comfort of a home office. But working as a writer is much broader than what you might imagine. Famous novelists are just one of the most prominent types of writers, but there are also journalists, nonfiction writers, children's book writers, and bloggers. You can write plays or movie scripts. The possibilities within writing are endless. You can also work within the publishing industry without actually being a writer yourself. There are jobs for people with a sharp eye for grammar, design skills, or research. And a good number of writing jobs don't require college, simply a talent for words and an understanding of the business. Recently, many

Working as a writer can be very rewarding, but the career path requires devotion, dedication, and a tireless attitude, even in the face of rejection.

of these jobs have moved online as well, allowing you to work from anywhere or even get your writing career started right now, today.

Good writers are necessary in almost every industry. Being able to communicate clearly and effectively is a skill that can take you places. In the following fifteen sections, we'll take a look at several individual career paths that you can explore if you have a talent for or interest in writing. And the best part is that none of them require getting a college education, so if you're worried about student loans or debt, then you're already on the right track to finding a career in writing!

CHAPTER 1

FICTION WRITER/NOVELIST

If you're the type of person who loves telling stories, is creative, and finds joy in sitting down at a computer or notebook to jot down your latest short story or poem, then you might have what it takes to be a fiction writer or novelist. Becoming a novelist is among the most difficult challenges for a writer. If you like writing, however, and don't mind the time and diligence it requires to develop characters and plots, then writing a novel can be satisfying and inspirational.

WHAT THEY DO

In order to become a successful novelist, you must first be devoted to it. Practice is essential to becoming a novelist. You must write (and read) constantly, or at the very least, regularly. Reading is the best way to improve as a writer. For every word in a novel, the author may have written ten others that were revised.

A novelist's approach to his or her job is an individual one. Some novelists set aside a certain time of the day or week to write; others go at it in spurts. Some novelists treat writing as a full-time job. Others will write as little as two pages a day; at this rate they would produce more than seven hundred pages of first-draft material in one year. Still, all writers revise their work, which can also be time-consuming. Some novelists revise once or twice, while others revise for years. Writing any novel takes a considerable amount of time. Most authors will work on a novel for a minimum of one to three years. The most important thing for a novelist is to establish a writing regimen and maintain it.

It is also important to research the novel market frequently and to stay on top of the latest news about the publishing industry. When a writer finishes a novel, he or she submits it to an agent or publisher. The manuscript must be typed and formatted according to industry standards and the specific guidelines of the publisher.

PREPARING FOR YOUR CAREER

There are a lot of novelists who never graduated from college—Louisa May Alcott, Ernest Hemingway, and James Baldwin, just to name just a few. While a formal education can certainly help you develop any writing career, becoming a novelist is often more dependent on personality and a drive to succeed. You can start to develop many of the skills necessary to become a novelist in high school. Writers write about what they know and understand. Even fantasy and science fiction writers use experiences from their lives to create characters, plots, dialogue, and themes.

Writers always look for chances to learn new things. When asked by aspiring authors for advice, many established writers tell them to read as much as possible. Reading a variety of texts, from novels to newspaper articles, will strengthen your knowledge of vocabulary and grammar and will educate you about a wide range of topics. You will also encounter an abundance of styles, which will help you find you own.

JOB OUTLOOK AND SALARY

Publishing a novel can be a financially rewarding experience, if you can get through the hard

Louisa May Alcott, the author of *Little Women*, was praised for creating warm and interesting characters, based on the people in her own life. Jo March, the heroine of *Little Women*, was based on Alcott herself.

work of writing a good novel. You may sell your first novel for $10,000 to $50,000, and you may receive more money if the book does well or when the paperback edition is printed. In 2004, British novelist J. K. Rowling earned close to $200 million, making her the highest-paid novelist in history. Today, she's worth more than $1 billion.

Once you've submitted your work to an agent or publisher, the waiting game begins. It can take months to receive a response from a publisher; and you may never receive a response. Rejection letters are sure to pile up before you receive a positive response, and a positive response does not necessarily mean that your work will even be published. Many people yearn to establish a career as a novelist, but a mere fraction of those people achieve their dream.

Writing novels, however, is much like any other art form. Most artists don't think of their art as a way to earn money. Novelists write because they enjoy it. The best advice to an aspiring novelist is perhaps also the harshest: plan on establishing a career as a novelist while you earn money doing something else. Many careers allow novelists to perfect their professional writing skills while also writing for pleasure.

FOR MORE INFORMATION

ORGANIZATIONS

The Authors Guild
31 E 32nd Street, 7th Floor
New York, NY 10016
(212) 563-5904
Website: http://www.authorsguild.org
The Authors Guild is the nation's oldest and largest
   professional organization for writers. Since its
   beginnings over a century ago, it has served as the
   collective voice of American authors.

Canadian Authors Association (CAA)
6 West Street N, Suite 203
Orillia, ON L3V 5B8
Canada
(705) 325-3926
Website: http://canadianauthors.org/national
The Canadian Authors Association provides writers
   with a wide variety of programs, services, and
   resources to help them develop their skills in both
   the craft and the business of writing, enhance their
   ability to earn a living as a writer, and have access to

a Canada-wide network of writers and publishing industry professionals.

BOOKS

King, Stephen. *On Writing: 10th Anniversary Edition: A Memoir of the Craft.* New York, NY: Scribner, 2010.
Lamott, Anne. *Bird by Bird: Some Instructions on Writing and Life.* New York, NY: Anchor, 1995.

PERIODICALS

Writer's Digest
4700 E. Galbraith Road
Cincinnati, OH 45236
(513) 531-2222
Website: http://www.writersdigest.com

WEBSITES

Because of the changing nature of internet links, Rosen Publishing has developed an online list of websites related to the subject of this book. This site is updated regularly. Please use this link to access the list:

http://www.rosenlinks.com/CCWC/writing

CHAPTER 2

EDITOR

Writing is only the first step of the process. From there, an editor or editorial team shapes the writing so that it is a perfect fit for the intended audience. While they may not always receive as much credit, editors are just as important as writers in the world or publishing.

WHAT THEY DO

Editors correct errors in text and prepare manuscripts for layout and design. That is just a basic description of an editor's duties. Editors actually have many responsibilities. Newspaper editors ensure articles are written objectively and that they are not too difficult for the average reader. Book editors read and edit more text on a daily basis than do newspaper editors, but they must be more sensitive to the writer's original intent. It is not necessarily book editors' job to write or rewrite the text that is given to them. Instead, they update the writing through the revision process while being sensitive to a writer's ideas and style as they shape the finished book. Magazine editors are often a mix between newspaper and book editors. Their duties vary depending on the type of writing they are working with: fiction, nonfiction, biographies, columns, and so on. Editors for online publications might also add coding to the text to add clickable elements like links.

Editors are sometimes required to create text, whether it's captions and sidebars for a news article or whole sections of a book. Other duties that editors may be required to handle include commissioning authors, securing copyrights, obtaining the right to use materials

Editors spend a lot of time in front of the computer, editing text, keeping up with correspondence, and working hard to keep projects on track.

created by other companies, research, contacting consultants and experts, updating previously written or outdated material, assigning projects to writers, and working with artists and designers.

Most publishing companies have an editorial staff. Senior or managing editors manage teams of editors. Assistant editors work under senior editors and are usually assigned projects. They must make important decisions about how the finished text will look, even though managing editors usually make the final decisions. In smaller companies, an editorial assistant may function as writer, editor, copy editor, and fact checker for a single project.

INSIDE THE STYLE GUIDE

Style guides (sometimes known as stylebooks) are vital tools for publishers. They ensure that the entire company adheres to a single set of language rules, which helps writers and editors to avoid contradictions and errors. Most publishers use established style guides, such as *The Associated Press Stylebook* or *The Chicago Manual of Style*. Others create their own style guides that work in conjunction with an established guide. Style guides cover rules of grammar, punctuation, capitalization, proofreader's marks, abbreviations, regional expressions, footnote techniques, and much more.

Many editors earn high figures as freelancers. They advertise their services in print and online. Some offer general editing services, while others are specialists who edit one kind of writing, such as fiction, term papers, medical texts, and so on.

PREPARING FOR YOUR CAREER

One of the first and most important things that editors need is a solid understanding of the English language. Many of the things you need to know to become an editor you will learn on the job. Publishers and online publications usually have their own set of standards and guidelines for their employees to follow, but the skills that you learn editing for one company will certainly be useful when working for another. Employers expect editors to be excellent communicators and to read, evaluate, and correct text quickly.

Many publishers produce books on a limited range of topics. The same can be said of online publications with all articles falling under a specific umbrella, like tech subjects, beauty, or lifestyle. If you choose to work for a publisher like this, it will be beneficial to learn all you can about the topic or topics in which your publisher specializes. The more knowledge you have the easier your job will become. On the other hand, some publishers produce works on a

INTERVIEW WITH AN EDITOR

Dan Meyer was the editor of the *Sun & Erie County Independent* of Hamburg, New York for many years. He has also worked as a newspaper reporter.

WHAT DO YOU LIKE BEST ABOUT YOUR JOB?

Every day is different. No two days are ever alike. One day I could be interviewing a police officer about a fatal car accident and then two hours later talking to a woman upset that the garbage company didn't pick up her trash. Then, later that night, I can be taking photographs at a Little League baseball game and then the next morning conducting an interview with a 100-year-old nun.

WHAT DO YOU LIKE LEAST ABOUT IT?

I dislike the paperwork associated with being editor—handling payroll forms, freelance writing bills, answering e-mail questions about why someone didn't receive their paycheck yet. Although I don't do the actual billing, I have to approve everything and then submit it to our payroll department and that takes time.

HOW IS WRITING IMPORTANT TO YOUR JOB?

Writing is extremely important. I have to be able to tell a story through my writing, whether it is a police report, a news article on the proposed school budget, or a high school football game review. Without strong writing skills, I would not be able to do my job.

(continued on the next page)

(continued from the previous page)

WHAT ADVICE WOULD YOU GIVE TO SOMEONE THINKING ABOUT PURSUING A JOURNALISM CAREER?
Keep an open mind. Stay informed by reading your local newspapers, the daily newspaper, *USA Today*, etc. Watch the local TV news every day and listen to local talk radio. Be prepared to work odd hours and be flexible. Try and be a good listener and strive to be a good "people person."

wide range of topics. Whatever the case, it helps to be well read and knowledgeable. The more you know, the easier it will be to "sell" yourself to an employer.

JOB OUTLOOK AND SALARY

Editors make an average salary of $56,010 but may make more depending on their level of experience. An editor starting out in the field (as an editorial assistant or assistant editor) should expect his or her salary to be around $30,000, sometimes lower depending on the job location. These numbers may be similar for freelance editors, depending on the kind of work they find and how often they find it. Senior editors, executive editors, and editorial directors can make between $40,000 and $150,000 or more depending on their level of experience and the size of the publisher for whom they work.

Editors are vital to the publishing industry. However, there are other industries that also need editors. Any company that produces printed materials—such as newsletters, advertisements, reports, and so on—need editors to make sure that those materials convey their messages clearly and without errors. There are plenty of career options for both staff and freelance editors.

FOR MORE INFORMATION

ORGANIZATIONS

American Society of News Editors (ASNE)
209 Reynolds Journalism Institute
Missouri School of Journalism
Columbia, MO 65211
(573) 882-2430
Website: http://www.asne.org
The American Society of News Editors is a nonprofit
   professional organization that promotes fair,
   principled journalism, defends and protects First
   Amendment rights, and fights for freedom of
   information and open government.

The Association of Magazine Media
757 Third Avenue, 11th floor
New York, NY 10017
(212) 872-3700
Website: http://www.magazine.org
Established in 1919, the Association of Magazine Media
   is the primary advocate and voice for the magazine
   media industry.

Editorial Freelancers Association (EFA)
71 West 23rd Street, 4th floor

New York, NY 10010

(212) 929-5400

Website: http://www.the-efa.org

This nonprofit organization provides networking and
support for freelance editors in the US and abroad.

BOOKS

Dunham, Steve. *The Editor's Companion: An Indispensable
Guide to Editing Books, Magazines, Online Publications,
and More.* Ft. Collins, CO: Writers Digest, 2014.

Strunk, William, Jr. *The Elements of Style.* Needham
Heights, MA: Allyn & Bacon, 1979.

University of Chicago Press Staff. *The Chicago Manual
of Style, 16th ed.* Chicago, IL: University of Chicago
Press, 2010.

WEBSITES

Because of the changing nature of internet links, Rosen
Publishing has developed an online list of websites
related to the subject of this book. This site is updated
regularly. Please use this link to access the list:

http://www.rosenlinks.com/CCWC/writing

CHAPTER 3

REVIEWER

Do you like movies or checking out the latest tech? Do you love to read the newest books? Are you a music fanatic? Are you someone who enjoys dining at the latest restaurants? If you are a writer who enjoys music, films, plays, books, or fine dining, you might consider becoming a critic or reviewer. Not only is writing about entertainment fun, it's a career with plenty of perks: free film and theater tickets; tons of music, movies, computer software, and demos; copies of books long before they are released to the public; and swarms of people rushing to bring you the finest fare they have to offer. Sound good? Read on.

WHAT THEY DO

Reviewers tend to stick with a specific topic within their field. They write with style and authority. Knowledge of industry trends in the following categories is often necessary to become a critical reviewer: contemporary publishing; the music industry; theatrical entertainment and dance; film;

fashion and retailing; restaurants and cooking; technology; automobiles; and much more. Your can be a freelance or a staff reviewer. Some reviews are even syndicated.

Critics and reviewers have strong opinions, though that isn't enough to excel in this profession. Readers are more likely to respect your opinions when you can offer a keen insight into how you formed them. Can you compare a band's new release to its earlier catalog of titles? How about the latest software? How is it better or worse than the company's earlier version? Critics and reviewers rely on their extensive knowledge to back up their opinions. It isn't enough to say that the new album by Taylor Swift is excellent or horrible; you must know enough about music, songwriting, and the music

Restaurant reviewers have a job to do when they sit down to a meal in a restaurant. They not only assess the quality of the food but the quality of the service as well.

industry to explain why it is either a groundbreaking or a repeat performance.

In addition to individual expertise, both critics and reviewers need to develop effective writing skills and an authoritative and persuasive voice. As in any other writing career, publishers will turn down your review if it contains spelling errors, grammatical mistakes, or formatting problems.

Once you sell your first review, others will generally follow. Many freelancers use their first few reviews as a foundation for new publishing clients. Successful reviewers also often receive comps. These are giveaways such as electronics, books, film and theater tickets, and free downloads from companies that are hoping for favorable press and the chance to obtain some free promotion.

Sometimes critics must deal with hard feelings from readers. Some readers will agree with your opinions; others will not. Regularly on web forums, readers are offended when they read negative reviews about their favorite artists. As any critic will reveal, some readers respond to critics with unkind messages or comments. Negative response is difficult to avoid when you are a critic. If your work is published online, your web administrator will have the task of keeping an eye on comments and making sure they don't get out of hand.

PREPARING FOR YOUR CAREER

While critics do not require a college degree, they do need to be experts in their chosen field. You can achieve this expertise through a combination of methods. First and most important, you need to immerse yourself in the area about which you want to write. If you want to be a reviewer of plays, for example, you need to attend as many theatrical performances as you can. If you like to follow trends in fashion, attend as many fashion shows as you can, and so on. In general, all potential critics should learn as much as possible in their chosen fields. Read books by experts. Watch related movies and documentaries. Speak with established professionals. Attend workshops.

Theater critics must be well versed in modern theater. They keep an eye on trends and see all the latest shows.

To become more familiar with authoritative and persuasive writing styles, select four or five critics and read as many of their reviews as possible. Choose a few critics you like and a couple you dislike. Pay attention to the ideas on which all the reviews focus and the descriptive terms they use to describe those ideas. The knowledge you gain from reading published work will help you create your own individual writing style later.

JOB OUTLOOK AND SALARY

Depending on the publication, freelance reviewers with slight experience may make as little as $25 a review. Other writers who have honed their skills and published reviews in a few magazines, newspapers, or online publications may make $300 or more. A reviewer with a regular column could make $30,000, $40,000, or more.

A career as a critic or reviewer is more specialized than a career as a news reporter, and the positions can be especially hard to come by because there are so few of them in print publications. Online publications provide for a little more flexibility. Writing reviews for an online publication might just be one part of your job. Your success in this specialized writing field depends on your overall experience as a writer and your knowledge of what you are reviewing.

WORK ENVIRONMENT

Critics and reviewers—regardless of their areas of expertise—must immerse themselves in their work. If you are a critic of popular films, you must see just about every movie that appears in the theaters and perhaps also movies that are available exclusively through streaming services. Book reviewers read books constantly and quickly. Restaurant critics eat at different restaurants on a weekly or daily basis. Tech reviewers continually purchase (or receive) electronic devices in order to test them out and write reviews.

In many respects, critics and reviewers are fortunate to be paid to do exactly what they like to do, whether that's eating out, reading new books, listening to new music, or seeing new films. Keep in mind, however, that unless you truly love the area you've chosen to work in, there is a chance that you may grow tired of doing one thing all the time. In short, make sure you love what you do before deciding to make it your career; otherwise you may burn out.

Many reviewers and critics begin as freelance writers working for small town papers. After a while, their editors may offer them a chance to write a review. They gain more experience and make the transition to larger newspapers and magazines. Online reviewers might just discover they have a knack for it. As with any writing career, determination, persistence, and a thick skin will help you succeed.

FOR MORE INFORMATION

ORGANIZATIONS

American Library Association
50 East Huron Street
Chicago, IL 60611
(800) 545-2433
Website: http://www.ala.org
The American Library Association (ALA) is the oldest
and largest library association in the world.

BOOKS

Jones, Chris. *Bigger, Brighter, Louder: 150 Years of Chicago Theater as Seen by "Chicago Tribune" Critics*. Chicago, IL: University of Chicago Press, 2013.

Lawrence, Sylvester. *Food Critic Mastery: How to Judge and Write About Food Like a Professional Food Critic*. Seattle, WA: Amazon Digital, 2014.

Maltin, Leonard. *Turner Classic Movies Presents Leonard Maltin's Classic Movie Guide: From the Silent Era Through 1965*, 3rd ed. New York, NY: Plume, 2015.

Null, Christopher. *Five Stars! How to Become a Film Critic, the World's Greatest Job*. San Francisco, CA: Sutro Press, 2013.

PERIODICALS

Booklist
The American Library Association
50 East Huron Street
Chicago, IL 60611
(800) 545-2433
Website: http://www.ala.org/booklist

WEBSITES

Because of the changing nature of internet links, Rosen Publishing has developed an online list of websites related to the subject of this book. This site is updated regularly. Please use this link to access the list:

http://www.rosenlinks.com/CCWC/writing

CHAPTER 4

PUBLIC RELATIONS ASSISTANT

The public reputation of a company or public figure is extremely important. If an organization or politician does something that looks bad in the eyes of the public, this can create an online firestorm that can cause permanent damage. Needless to say, this is the opposite of what a company or politician wants. In these cases, powerful public relations can work wonders to save a company from going under or get a politician elected to office.

WHAT THEY DO

Public relations assistants communicate directly with the public or the media for the purpose of expressing opinions, policies, or responses to public concerns. They also receive and respond to complaints made by members of the public or by public service organizations. It is public relations assistants' job to present the company or individual for whom they work in a favorable light. They are also sometimes needed to repair reputations that have been damaged in the eyes of the public.

Anyone or any group that is interested in portraying a positive image to the general public may hire a public relations assistant. They work for public figures, politicians, government agencies, companies, advertising agencies, associations, nonprofit organizations, colleges, television stations, and hospitals. Some public relations assistants work for consulting firms and are assigned to cover individual events for clients. Others might be specialists in a specific area, such as children's groups or sports figures.

Public relations assistants usually report to public relations managers or executives. The executives are those workers who are in direct contact with company management. The executives relay information to the assistants and inform them how to proceed. In many cases, the executives receive the credit for the work that public relations assistants accomplish. For instance, executives may give speeches written by assistants or they may use copy written by assistants in press conferences.

Public relations assistants need solid writing skills. In many ways, the public relations assistant is much like a copywriter. Both must "sell" their company and its goods and/or services. Public relations specialists write text for speeches, press releases, newsletters, advertisements, shareholder reports, employee handbooks, magazine articles, and more.

In addition to these duties, public relations assistants may be required to schedule fund-raisers, give speeches and interviews, organize meetings and conventions, investigate complaints, mediate discussions, and create promotional and training videos. Public relations workers need to be familiar with modern business practices, have excellent communications skills, and be good leaders.

PREPARING FOR YOUR CAREER

While many employers prefer that public relations assistants have a college degree, it isn't always necessary. Experience in journalism, copy writing, or advertising may often lead to a position as a public relations assistant.

You can prepare for a public relations job in high school by working for your school newspaper and/or television station. Volunteering to help on political campaigns may also help. While you are still in high school, having a retail job can help you form solid selling techniques. Many public relations assistants begin their careers as news reporters or as interns and administrative assistants for public relations firms.

Public relations workers who have been working in the field for five years can take a certification course that is administered by the Public Relations Society of America.

By doing this, you can use the term "Accredited in Public Relations" when describing your experience.

JOB OUTLOOK AND SALARY

An entry-level public relations assistant salary may start as low as $25,000, depending on experience and job location. However, this number usually increases quickly, especially after the assistnat has proven him- or herself as a competent writer. The average salary for public relations workers falls at around $56,770 with a 6 percent increase of job availability through 2024.

Individuals looking for work in the public relations field are often assigned low-responsibility duties, such as taking polls or collecting research. Moving up the ladder may take some time because the skills you need take time to master. The more experience you have, the more responsibility you will receive. Some public relations assistants wait for promotions at the company for which they work, while others prefer to change companies when they have gained sufficient experience. If you gain enough knowledge and expertise in a specific field you may decide to become an independent consultant. This option, however, takes a great deal of experience. The good news is that there are thousands of companies that require public relations workers of every level.

FOR MORE INFORMATION

ORGANIZATIONS

Institute for Public Relations (IPR)
PO Box 118400
2096 Weimer Hall
Gainesville, FL 32611-8400
(352) 92-0280
Website: http://www.instituteforpr.com
The Institute for Public Relations (IPR) is a nonprofit
foundation dedicated to research in, on, and for
public relations.

Public Relations Society of America
120 Wall Street, 21st floor
New York, NY 10005
(212) 460-1400
Website: http://www.prsa.org
PRSA provides professional development, sets
standards of excellence, and upholds principles of
ethics for its members.

BOOKS

Petrov, Kosta D., and Jonathan A.J. Wilson, eds. *The
Little Black Book of PR: Mastering Public Relations in a
Changing World*. Skopje, Macedonia: P World, 2016.

Scott, David Meerman. *The New Rules of Marketing and PR: How to Use Social Media, Online Video, Mobile Applications, Blogs, News Releases, and Viral Marketing to Reach Buyers Directly*. Hoboken, NJ: Wiley, 2015.

WEBSITES

Because of the changing nature of internet links, Rosen Publishing has developed an online list of websites related to the subject of this book. This site is updated regularly. Please use this link to access the list:

http://www.rosenlinks.com/CCWC/writing

CHAPTER 5

COPY EDITOR

Spelling errors are everywhere. Would you buy a television from a store after reading a sign in its window that said, "No won can beet our prices!" Perhaps you would—especially if the prices really were unbeatable—but chances are you would think twice about buying anything from a store that couldn't spell the words on its own sign. Writing copy is

Copy editors must assess the grammar of a piece of writing, smooth the flow of the text, and check it to make sure that everything makes sense.

a job for copywriters. Correcting and perfecting that copy is a job for copy editors.

This career is best for people who are knowledgeable, determined, and passionate about everything they do—especially copyediting. This is a job for individuals who make informed, sensible decisions, and then stand by those decisions. That is not to say that copy editors won't admit when they are wrong, but they are seldom wrong, and they know it.

WHAT THEY DO

Copy editors work for book publishers, magazines, online publications, and newspapers. Also, nearly every company that creates advertisements uses copy editors. They make sure that the writing for soon-to-be published pieces is as accurate and as factual as possible. Copy editors examine spelling, grammar, style, and the slant of the writing. Copy editors work quickly and efficiently, and they must have good communication skills.

Copy editors must have a strong understanding of the industry in which they work, as well as the style guide and practices of the company for whom they work. A newspaper copy editor should know how to write headlines and captions. Copy editors who work for a book publisher might need to know how to create an index. In other words, they need to become familiar with the entire publishing process. Many copy editors are expected to be familiar with typesetting commands, which they often write directly in the margins of the piece of writing they are copyediting. But typesetting marks are used less often as the publishing process goes digital.

Equally important is a sense of curiosity. Copy editors always want to know more, and they spend a good deal of time researching and exploring a wide range of topics—even in their spare time. This constant pursuit of knowledge is what makes copy editors good at what they do. Vital to a copy editor's job is a wide range of reference materials: dictionaries, encyclopedias, atlases, online wikis, stylebooks, and many others.

Many employers like to hire copy editors who can offer creative suggestions on how to correct errors. This could mean changing a few words or rewriting an entire paragraph. In this instance, your creativity could help save time and meet a deadline. Copy editors often make suggestions for the design team as well.

Copyediting is often thought of as a thankless job. It is their job to point out changes that need to be made at a time late in the production schedule, after editors and writers have crafted what they think is a well-written and flawless piece of writing. Nevertheless, copy editors thrive on being anned for breakfast, sitting under the huge green ich had been set up outside the café on the upper

was

ll early in the morning, the sun already blazing

ze was spiced with the scent of riv life, but thi

ground c

Copy editors use proofreading marks to point out and fix mistakes. They use brightly colored writing utensils so that the changes are hard to miss!

detail-oriented professionals who know the obscure rules of grammar and language. They notice the minor errors that others are too busy to see.

When applying for a job as a copy editor, it is important to know something about the publication to which you are applying. If you are applying for a job at a newspaper, for example, be sure to read as many copies of the paper as possible. Become familiar with the layout, the columns, and the writers. The same goes for magazine and book publishers and online publications. Familiarize yourself with the company and its product.

PREPARING FOR YOUR CAREER

Most employers require professional experience from their copy editors. This is not always the case, as long as you

PROOFREADING SYMBOLS

The following chart shows a sample of common symbols and abbreviations traditionally used by copy editors to convey information to editors, writers, and designers. These symbols are written directly on printed proofs, usually in the margins, and are meant as directions for revision. Some modernized publishers, however, have copy editors make changes digitally, using a track changes function.

symbol	meaning	symbol	meaning
	insert text or punctuation		paragraph
	delete		delete and close space
(three lines) or cap	capitalize		close up space
L.C.	lowercase	#	insert space
=	insert hyphen	Stet	leave text as it is
sp	check spelling	or tr	transpose (reverse) letters/words

have strong language skills, enthusiasm for your job, and a willingness to learn. Employers who are looking for a copy editor often want someone who is thorough, confident, and knowledgeable about everyday events.

Some companies will expect you to have experience with design and editing programs. Not all, however, will expect this type of experience, and many will even teach you specific software programs on the job.

JOB OUTLOOK AND SALARY

Copy editors average a salary between $20,000 and $58,000. But many copy editors are hired as freelancers and can set an hourly (or per word) wage according to the company for which they are working. Some freelance copy editors work for several companies at a time.

Nearly every book publisher, magazine, and newspaper has at least one copy editor, though most have an entire department or team of copy editors, so job openings in certain industries are plentiful. However, competition for these jobs can be fierce, though adept copy editors can work their way up to copy chief or managing editor if they set their minds to it.

FOR MORE INFORMATION

ORGANIZATIONS

American Copy Editors Society (ACES)
11690B Sunrise Valley Drive
Reston, VA 20191-1409
(703) 453-1122
Website: http://www.copydesk.org
ACES, the American Copy Editors Society, is a nonprofit
education and membership organization working
toward the advancement of copy editors.

Modern Language Association (MLA)
85 Broad Street, Suite 500
New York, NY 10004
(646) 576-5000
Website: http://www.mla.org
The Modern Language Association of America provides
opportunities for its members to share their scholarly
findings and teaching experiences with colleagues
and to discuss trends in the academy.

BOOKS

Dunham, Steve. *The Editor's Companion: An Indispensable Guide to Editing Books, Magazines, Online Publications, and More*. Ft. Collins, CO: Writers Digest, 2014.

Einsohn, Amy. *The Copyeditor's Handbook: A Guide for Book Publishing and Corporate Communications.* Oakland, CA: University of California Press, 2011.

Saller, Carol Fisher. *The Subversive Copy Editor: Advice from Chicago*, 2nd ed. Chicago, IL: University of Chicago Press, 2016.

Strunk, William, Jr. *The Elements of Style.* Needham Heights, MA: Allyn & Bacon, 1979.

University of Chicago Press Staff. *The Chicago Manual of Style*, 16th ed. Chicago, IL: University of Chicago Press, 2010.

WEBSITES

Because of the changing nature of internet links, Rosen Publishing has developed an online list of websites related to the subject of this book. This site is updated regularly. Please use this link to access the list:

http://www.rosenlinks.com/CCWC/writing

CHAPTER 6

PRINT JOURNALIST

On your way to work one morning you get a call from your managing editor. Surprise calls from her are nothing new because you work for a local newspaper. You have to rush downtown, where a congressman is giving an impromptu speech to his constituents about pollution issues in the state. Even though you have never met the man, it is your job to prepare questions, get an interview, and report the facts. Timing is everything. Your job depends on getting the story quickly and making a good impression. Being a newspaper reporter can be an exciting and hectic job because you have to be ready for anything.

There are thousands of newspapers in the United States, all of them varying in size and scope. Whether they are serving big cities or small towns, all newspapers need reporters to investigate events and write about them every day. Depending on how big the company is, a newspaper may have hundreds of reporters or just a few.

Political journalists are invited to press conferences held by important political figures, like the president.

WHAT THEY DO

Newspaper reporters work alongside managing editors, copy editors, and others to investigate a topic or event and write about it. Reporters gather facts about various happenings, including community events, political developments, and crimes. Some reporters specialize in specific topics, such as sporting events or community meetings. Beat reporters often cover stories that occur in the same location—their beat—such as hospitals, schools, and courthouses. Most newspapers also depend on freelance writers and reporters, who are commonly called stringers. Stringers often investigate and report news events that occur in areas outside the local community or pursue less time-sensitive stories that "fill out" the paper when the news is slow.

Authoritative interviewing techniques and accurate note taking are two vital components of news reporting. Learning shorthand allows writers to take notes quickly. Although many reporters still use pen and paper to gather the facts, most reporters use recorders to help them get the story. Some even carry cameras with them to take photos, or they may work closely with a professional photographer who is also assigned to the story.

Once reporters have completed their research, conducted interviews, and gathered as many facts as possible within a given period, they can begin writing an article. Reporters might also use other resources, including reference materials, court documents, public records, and the internet. Reporters must think and write objectively about their topics. It is important to report the facts of a story without allowing personal opinions to affect the angle of the article. Reporters often use a priority system to help them decide which facts are most important in a story. In short, a reporter's main job is to write about situations or events in simple, precise language that the average reader can understand.

Reporters also have to meet daily or weekly deadlines. After a final proofing, reporters turn in their work to a senior or managing editor who then reads the piece and often makes comments about it. The managing editor may or may not ask the reporter to change words or phrases. Sometimes managing editors make those changes themselves.

GLOSSARY OF JOURNALISM

byline—The name of the writer appearing at the top of an article.

caption—Text that accompanies a photograph, illustration, graph, or chart.

dateline—A line of text at the beginning of an article that gives the location and time the piece was written.

feature—An article of prominence in a newspaper.

lead—The first one to three paragraphs of a story. Pronounced "leed," but sometimes spelled "lede" to avoid confusion with the metal.

masthead—The name and logo of the newspaper that appears at the top of page one. Sometimes called the flag or nameplate.

sidebar—Additional information that accompanies an article but is set apart from the regular text. This text is often placed in a box, and for this reason sidebars are sometimes simply called boxes.

Reporters must be able to work quickly and skillfully to meet recurring deadlines, which can sometimes be just a few hours after receiving an assignment. To meet demanding deadlines, some reporters relay their stories to editors over the phone or through e-mail.

News reporting is a demanding job. Busy newsrooms, challenging deadlines, frequent research, and dangerous assignments can cause a great deal of stress for any writer. If you like excitement and activity, however, writing for a newspaper might be the perfect job for you. The harder you work, the more exciting your assignments will be—and the more pay you will receive.

PREPARING FOR YOUR CAREER

Communication, writing, and keyboarding skills are a must for news reporters. Big city newspapers—such as the *Chicago Tribune* and the *New York Times*—often hire only college graduates. However, newspapers serving small towns and local communities will hire a reporter based on his or her writing skills or past work experience. Personal qualities like curiosity, dedication, and determination are also extremely important. Small-town papers are more likely to hire someone straight out of high school than are larger newspapers serving a larger city or region.

The *New York Times*, founded in 1851, is one of the most respected newspapers in the world. In 1865, the *Times* ran a front cover story covering the death of Abraham Lincoln.

Many reporters gain experience and confidence at smaller papers and then move on to bigger papers and better positions. Newspaper publishers consider past experience a valuable asset. Even working on your school newspaper or yearbook will help you gain some of the experience necessary for a writing career. Writing for television and radio news programs can also prepare you for a career as a newspaper reporter.

WHAT IS A NEWS AGENCY?

News agencies are organizations supported by journalists with the intention of supplying breaking and continuous news reports to other news outlets, such as newspapers, television and radio news shows, and news-related websites. Most agencies supply a variety of media—including photographs, audio clips, and videotape footage—in addition to written news reports. A cooperative is a news agency that is owned and operated by the newspapers that contribute stories to it; these newspapers share the stories contributed to or written by the agency. Other news agencies are corporations that sell their news stories to other news venues. The Associated Press (AP) and Reuters are the two largest English-based news agencies in the world. AP is an American cooperative that claims to be the world's oldest and largest news agency. As of 2005, 1,700 newspapers and 5,000 television and radio outlets were members of AP. *The Associated Press Stylebook* has become the standard writing guide for American journalism. Reuters is a European news agency that sells news stories and financial information to news companies all over the world. Reuters currently functions in ninety-one countries and in eighteen languages.

JOB OUTLOOK AND SALARY

Novice freelance or staff reporters can expect to make between $15,000 and $30,000 a year. More experienced reporters may make an average of $37,720 a year. Freelancers and stringers are paid based on the size and type of articles they write, the publication for which they write, and their level of experience.

News reporting is a competitive field with many opportunities. Reporters usually work forty hours a week or more. Most are not compensated for overtime work. Many reporters spend nights and weekends reading or doing research to follow a story or to gain more insight on a topic. Being a print journalist is also becoming increasingly challenging because news is moving to the internet. Many newspapers are shutting down or cutting staff. So gaining experience in technology is vital.

News writers gain recognition with time by writing for larger publications that reach wider audiences. Some news writers have the potential to become newspaper editors, even assistant or managing editors.

FOR MORE INFORMATION

ORGANIZATIONS

Accuracy in Media (AIM)
4350 East West Highway, Suite 555
Bethesda, MD 20814
(202) 364-4401
Website: http://www.aim.org
Accuracy In Media is a nonprofit, grassroots citizens
   watchdog of the news media that critiques botched
   and bungled news stories and sets the record straight
   on important issues.

American Press Institute (API)
4401 Wilson Boulevard, Suite 900
Arlington, VA 22203
(571) 366-1200
Website: http://www.americanpressinstitute.org
The American Press Institute conducts research and
   training and creates tools to help chart a path for
   journalism in the twenty-first century.

American Society of Journalists and Authors
355 Lexington Avenue, 15th floor
New York, NY 10017-6603
(212) 997-0947

Website: http://www.asja.org
Founded in 1948, the American Society of Journalists
  and Authors is the nation's professional organization
  of independent nonfiction writers.

Fairness and Accuracy in Reporting (FAIR)
124 W. 30th Street, Suite 201
New York, NY 10001
(212) 633-6700
Website: http://www.fair.org
FAIR, the national media watch group, has been
  offering well-documented criticism of media bias and
  censorship since 1986.

Society of Professional Journalists
Eugene S. Pulliam National Journalism Center
3909 N. Meridian Street
Indianapolis, IN 46208
(317) 927-8000
Website: http://www.spj.org
The Society of Professional Journalists is the nation's
  most broad-based journalism organization, dedicated
  to encouraging the free practice of journalism and
  stimulating high standards of ethical behavior.

BOOKS

Kovach, Bill, and Tom Rosenstiel. *The Elements of Journalism: What Newspeople Should Know and the Public Should Expect*. New York, NY: Three Rivers Press, 2014.

Miller, Sally, and Gina Horkey. *Make Money as a Freelance Writer: 7 Simple Steps to Start Your Freelance Writing Business and Earn Your First $1,000*. Seattle, WA: Amazon Digital, 2016.

Petit, Zachary. *The Essential Guide to Freelance Writing: How to Write, Work, and Thrive on Your Own Terms*. Ft. Collins, CO: Writers Digest Press, 2015.

WEBSITES

Because of the changing nature of internet links, Rosen Publishing has developed an online list of websites related to the subject of this book. This site is updated regularly. Please use this link to access the list:

http://www.rosenlinks.com/CCWC/writing

CHAPTER 7

CHILDREN'S WRITER

Children's literature has been popular for hundreds of years. Everyone has a fond memory of a book they enjoyed as a child. In fact, it is believed that the ancient writer Aesop wrote his fables in the sixth century BCE. It seems that children's literature is here to stay, and many people have made a good living by writing for children.

WHAT THEY DO

The children's genre covers numerous types and styles of writing. Before setting out to establish a career as a children's author, you need to decide what you can offer to the children's market. Once you decide what you want to write, it will be easier to zero in on specific opportunities.

Children's magazines are extremely popular with kids, parents, and teachers. There are hundreds of freelance markets for children's magazine writers. Depending on the publication, these publishers are constantly looking for nonfiction articles, reviews, interviews, poems, and fiction.

Some children's magazines—such as *Highlights*—have readerships in the millions.

Children's books are equally well received. Despite the popularity of television, music, video games, and the internet, children's literature continues to be a successful business. Children are still reading classics like *Charlie and the Chocolate Factory* and *Charlotte's Web*. New children's "classics" such as the Harry Potter and Hunger Games series are extremely popular. The lasting appeal of children's literature is a benefit for those hoping to establish careers as writers.

Children's books are entertaining for children, are written in a way that appeals to a younger audience, and, perhaps most importantly, help readers work on their own reading skills.

In addition to children's fiction, there is a huge nonfiction market out there for children's writers. Schools and libraries are always searching for new books on a multitude of topics: science, social studies, biographies, the arts, sports, and more. Many book publishers specialize in library books for kids.

Despite this demand, the children's book and magazine market is extremely competitive. Editors simply don't have enough time to read all of the manuscripts that they receive. However, as with all writers who submit their work to editors, you can get published if you have solid ideas, can express them well, and know and follow the industry standards. (You can also look into finding an agent to represent your work to editors.) Writing the book or story is just half the battle. You also need to be mindful of the proper manuscript format, query style, submission guidelines, and so on. Pay attention to the market and be sure to read up on what's being currently published. These are the skills that will allow you to get your well-crafted story into the hands of an editor who will help you shape it for publication.

PREPARING FOR YOUR CAREER

A firm command of the English language is the first requirement of being a children's writer. Everything that you send to an editor—particularly your manuscript and query letter—should be free of errors and follow standard formatting guidelines.

Reading is always important for writers in all areas; the same is true for children's authors. It is important to understand the children's writers' market and know exactly whom you are writing for. Children's book writers should also read the latest children's books. This will help you develop your own unique style while keeping an eye on the market for what is popular and what is not.

JOB OUTLOOK AND SALARY

Payment for children's books varies greatly depending on the publisher and size of the book. You could make $100 or $50,000 for your first book, depending on the publisher, the length of the book, and the age range for which you are writing.

Depending on their popularity, children's magazines may pay as little as $25 for an article or story or as much as $1,000; they usually pay less for poetry. Some children's magazines only pay in copies. Be sure to read up on payment information (and rights) before submitting a piece of writing to a publication.

ROALD DAHL

Roald Dahl (1916–1990) will go down in history as one of the greatest children's writers of all time. His books are as popular today as they were when they were first released. While Dahl wrote many books for adults, it is his unique and quirky children's stories for which he is remembered.

Dahl had a difficult early life. Both of his parents died when he was very young. Dahl's stepmother raised him and his siblings in England. When he graduated high school, Dahl did not go to college. He first worked for an oil company and sailed on ships to Africa. When World War II began, he joined the Royal Air Force (RAF) and learned how to fly fighter planes. His very first flight ended in a crash in Libya. He survived to continue fighting for the English, but he left the RAF soon after due to medical reasons.

Dahl was sent to America in 1941 to help convince America to help England win the war. His first story, "Shot Down Over Libya," was published in the *Saturday Evening Post* in August 1942. This was the beginning of a long, celebrated career for Dahl.

Dahl knew how to entertain children. His stories are often creepy and grotesque, but they are always humorous. They tell the stories of lonely children, and they were written to make children laugh. Some of his greatest books include *Charlie and the Chocolate Factory*, *James and the Giant Peach*, *The BFG*, and *Matilda*. Dahl's long career is proof that children's writers can prosper without going to college, especially if they know how to think like children do.

Writing for children can be challenging yet rewarding. While starting out may be difficult, writing for magazines can help you to break into the book-publishing business. It can also help support you as you search for the right publisher for your book. Writing nonfiction can be just as pleasing and profitable as fiction. As with all writers who submit work to publishers, you should be prepared for a certain amount of rejection. This is especially true of first-time authors.

FOR MORE INFORMATION

ORGANIZATIONS

Society of Children's Book Writers & Illustrators (SCBWI)
4727 Wilshire Boulevard, Suite 301
Los Angeles, CA 90010
(323) 782-1010
Website: http://www.scbwi.org
The Society of Children's Book Writers and Illustrators, a
   nonprofit organization, is one of the largest existing
   organizations for writers and illustrators.

The Writers' Union of Canada
600-460 Richmond Street W.
Toronto, ON M5V 1Y1
Canada
(416) 703-8982
Website: http://www.writersunion.ca
The Writers' Union of Canada is the national
   organization of professionally published
   book authors.

BOOKS

Levine, Gail Carson. *Writing Magic: Creating Stories That
   Fly*. New York, NY: HarperCollins, 2014.

PERIODICALS

Horn Book Magazine
300 The Fenway
Palace Road Building, Suite P-311
Boston, MA 02115
Website: http://www.hbook.com

School Library Journal
123 William Street, Suite 802
New York, NY 10038
(646) 380-0700
Website: http://www.schoollibraryjournal.com

WEBSITES

Because of the changing nature of internet links, Rosen Publishing has developed an online list of websites related to the subject of this book. This site is updated regularly. Please use this link to access the list:

http://www.rosenlinks.com/CCWC/writing

CHAPTER 8

PARALEGAL OR LEGAL ASSISTANT

The legal profession is a growing, ever-changing industry. Lawyers are necessary for a long list of legal matters, from criminal trials to advising on business transactions. The duties that attorneys have are many, and our legal system would come to a grinding halt if it weren't for the hard work and dedication of paralegals.

WHAT THEY DO

Paralegals are also known as legal assistants. They assist lawyers in delivering legal services. Paralegals are seen as a necessary, time-saving component of our legal system. Lawyers usually take on the bulk of legal work, including interviewing clients and witnesses, giving legal advice, setting fees, accepting clients, and trying cases in a court of law. These are tasks for which legal assistants are not trained, and in fact it is against the law for them to carry out these activities.

However, these are just a few of the duties related to legal work. Paralegals complete a wide range of tasks that lawyers simply don't have time to complete on their own. In general,

Paralegals are skilled in legal proceedings and highly knowledgeable about the law.

paralegals help lawyers prepare for court cases, hearings, estate closings, will readings, and meetings. Some of the specific duties included in their job are researching past cases, investigating a current case to ensure the legal team has their facts straight, interviewing witnesses, analyzing and organizing information, and general administrative work.

Legal assistants sometimes interview clients and gather data about them under the supervision of a lawyer. Paralegal work almost always entails a long list of writing duties, including writing reports and letters, preparing legal arguments, and drafting contracts.

Law firms and government offices employ paralegals. They are also hired by corporations that have their own legal departments, such as Microsoft, United Airlines, and McDonalds, just to name a few. While the jobs of many paralegals often entail many or most of the duties listed in the previous paragraph, some tasks are more particular. Some legal assistants function more along the lines of an administrative assistant, with minimal legal work involved. Others specialize in a small area of legal work, such as preparing the necessary paperwork for real estate closings. Regardless of the focus of the job, writing skills are almost always a necessary requisite.

Paralegal jobs can be stressful. Deadlines for reports and projects are usually strict, and if the workload is large enough, legal assistants will be expected to work long hours. Some may be expected to travel frequently. Fortunately, most paralegals are rewarded for their hard work with excellent benefits, including vacation time and bonus pay. Despite the high level of stress related to paralegal jobs, they can also be exciting and fulfilling. Legal assistants meet many people and encounter many stories as they do their job.

PREPARING FOR YOUR CAREER

Some law firms require paralegals to have a college degree, but some are willing to train the right candidate on the job or even provide tuition. Since basic paralegal work is similar is some ways to secretarial work, gaining employment as a legal secretary or administrative assistant is excellent training. Many law firms offer on-the-job training. Those interested in becoming a paralegal can complete a paralegal certification program and receive the title registered paralegal, although most employers will not expect this certificate. (You can find more information about certification courses from the associations in the directory at the end of this chapter.) Still others may be hired because they have mastered a specific skill, such as experience filing tax returns.

JOB OUTLOOK AND SALARY

Salary for a paralegal depends on several criteria, including the size of the business or law firm, your training and experience, and the geographic location of the job. Beginning legal assistants may make about $30,000. Experienced paralegals may make up to $80,000 per year. The federal government is the largest employer of legal assistants in the United States and pays an average of about $63,720. Local and state governments pay legal assistants an average of $48,300.

Paralegal positions are numerous and are expected to remain so in the future. However, as mentioned previously, these jobs may be difficult to attain without a college degree. That does not mean you should give up hope of ever becoming a paralegal. Training in other jobs can help you to move up if you take the time to learn the skills necessary to work in a law office. A small number of paralegals are freelancers, although this is far from common in the industry.

FOR MORE INFORMATION

ORGANIZATIONS

Legal Secretaries International, Inc.
2951 Marina Bay Drive, Suite 130-641
League City, TX 77573
Website: http://www.legalsecretaries.org
Legal Secretaries International, Inc. was formed to
respond to the educational and networking needs of
legal secretaries as an affordable means of increasing
their knowledge, skills, and networking opportunities.

The National Association of Legal Assistants
7666 E. 61st Street, Suite 315
Tulsa, OK 74133
(918) 587-6828
Website: http://www.nala.org
NALA leads the paralegal profession by providing a
voluntary certification program, continuing legal
education, and professional development programs
for all paralegals.

The National Federation of Paralegal Associations
One Parkview Plaza, Suite 800
Oakbrook Terrace, IL 60181

(847) 686-2247
Website: http://www.paralegals.org
Founded in 1974, NFPA was the first national
   paralegal association.

BOOKS

Hatch, Scott A., and Lisa Zimmer Hatch. *Paralegal Career for Dummies*. Hoboken, NJ: For Dummies, 2011.

Miller, Roger LeRoy, and Mary Meinzinger. *Paralegal Today: The Essentials*. Independence, KY: Cengage, 2013.

WEBSITES

Because of the changing nature of internet links, Rosen Publishing has developed an online list of websites related to the subject of this book. This site is updated regularly. Please use this link to access the list:

http://www.rosenlinks.com/CCWC/writing

CHAPTER 9

MAGAZINE WRITER OR BLOGGER

Compared to news writing, magazine writing usually allows an author to write in a more individual and stylistic tone that reflects his or her own personal point of view. Magazine articles include interviews, book and film reviews, first-person accounts, essays, and more. Magazines also publish short works of fiction or excerpts from fiction and nonfiction books. Many national and regional magazines accept dozens of freelance articles from writers every month. This demand for well-crafted articles provides plenty of opportunities for hardworking magazine writers.

In the past several years, online publications have eclipsed magazine content for showcasing the latest interviews, reviews, and essays, although most magazines now have an online presence as well as a print format. Writing for an online publication is easier to break into because articles are published more often and there is a constant need for fresh, new content.

There are magazines for almost every subject. There are jobs in magazines for political journalists, fashion gurus, animal care workers, art experts, and so many more.

WHAT THEY DO

Magazine writers create the articles that fill the pages of periodicals. Some are in-house staffers who work for a single publication, but many work on a contract or freelance basis for a variety of publications. Successful magazine writers stay busy throughout the year. The more articles they write, the higher their salaries. Publishing a variety of articles enables freelance writers to earn a solid reputation, which will lead to more frequent assignments. Since they do not work under a supervisor's direction, freelance writers must remain focused on their schedule and deadlines.

Blogging for an online publication is very similar, although most writers of online content choose the freelance route because pay tends to be higher and it gives them the opportunity to write articles about a wider variety of topics regularly.

Freelance writers must be patient, yet persistent, when submitting their completed work or pitch for a story. It may be weeks or months after submitting an article or query (a letter or email sent by a writer to an editor or publisher to pitch his or her idea for a proposed article) that a writer receives word from a publisher. Once a writer has had his or her first articles published, this process usually becomes more fruitful. Editors who have already accepted an article from a freelance writer are usually more receptive to future work by the same author. If a freelance writer works hard enough, he or she may even secure a regular relationship with a magazine or online publication's editorial staff, often leading to more frequent and higher-paying projects.

One of the common mistakes freelance writers make is not becoming familiar with the publications or websites to which they submit their work. By reading a magazine from cover to cover, writers can familiarize themselves with the types of articles it prints and the style in which its articles are normally written. Successful freelance writers need to strive for a fresh, original approach to a subject matter that is often repeated.

The editors of specialized magazines such as *Men's Health* or *Cat Fancy*, for example, like to receive well-written articles that examine familiar topics in a new light. In addition, freelance writers need to follow a set of professional standards when submitting their work. In many cases, magazines set individual standards for submitted unsolicited articles. Follow these rules closely. If you don't, your work may not be considered, even if it is appropriate for publication.

PREPARING FOR YOUR CAREER

Having a college degree is not necessary if you want to write for a magazine or online publication, although life experience is invaluable. Successful writers adore the written word, love crafting a well-written piece, and have a sincere desire to impart information to readers. The language and writing skills that you learn in high school are important for a career as a writer. Other extracurricular activities such as writing for the yearbook or school newspaper may also be useful. Practice editing your own work for spelling, grammar, and punctuation errors and then have an English teacher proofread it.

Continually educating yourself both inside and outside the classroom is vital to a freelance writing career. Magazine writers often write about a wide variety of topics. Because of this, freelance writers need to be experts—or write like

A freelance magazine writer can more or less set her own hours and pitch articles across a variety of interests.

experts—about a great variety of topics. A mixture of good researching skills and effective writing habits will help you write articles that are both factual and engaging. Some writers, however, are actually experts on a particular subject. This requires learning all you can about the topic and staying up to date on developments in that field; after all, cutting-edge information often makes excellent content for the best magazine articles.

WRITING A QUERY LETTER

Making a good first impression is very important in publishing. Your first impression as a freelance writer is usually made in your query letter. Editors are very busy people, and they want to know that your work is worth their time. A good query letter (or query email) should be a brief but solid introduction to you and your ideas for the publication in which you would like to publish your work. Here is a brief list of important points to remember:

- Query letters should never be more than one printed page.
- The first half of your message should sell your article with a persuasive, concise description.
- The second half of your letter should sell you as a writer. Provide a brief list of the articles you have published and the magazines or online publications that have published them. If you have not yet been published, explain your experience with the topic of the article you are trying to sell.
- Mention if your article is a work in progress or a completed work. If incomplete, mention when you can send the finished piece to the editor.
- Don't forget to include your contact information: name, email address, and phone number.
- Proofread your query email for spelling and grammar mistakes.

JOB OUTLOOK AND SALARY

Payment for an article is based on several criteria, such as length (often measured by the word count), expertise, and the publication. Well-known periodicals—such as *Atlantic Monthly* or the *New Yorker*—often pay as much as $1,000 to $2,000 per article and sometimes more. Smaller publications and blogs offer much less compensation, perhaps between $10 and $300. Other publications only offer copies of the magazine as payment. Staff writers make between $20,000 and $65,000 a year and can establish lasting careers with single publications. Dedicated freelancers can make $20,000 a year or more, usually with a variety of publications. Some well-known freelancers make up to $500,000 a year.

People read magazines and blogs at home, at work, in medical facilities, in hair salons, in gyms, and in many other public places—any place you can find a Wi-Fi signal. Supermarket shelves and newsstands are packed with magazines on hundreds of topics from anthropology to zoology, and you can find articles on any subject online. If a freelance writer works hard enough, he or she can publish articles on a consistent basis. Some writers have full-time jobs and take freelance assignments on the side. Freelancing is a great way to supplement your income while building a name for yourself as a dependable writer.

FOR MORE INFORMATION

ORGANIZATIONS

Magazine Publishers of America (MPA)
757 Third Avenue, 11th floor
New York, NY 10017
Website: http://www.magazine.org
MPA is a nonprofit organization representing magazine media, print and digital. MPA provides an organized forum in which publishers can advance their common interests.

BOOKS

Brewer, Robert Lee. *2015 Writer's Market: The Most Trusted Guide to Getting Published*. Ft. Collins, CO: Writer's Digest, 2015.

James-Enger, Kelly. *Writer for Hire: 101 Secrets to Freelance Success*. Ft. Collins, CO: Writer's Digest, 2012.

Saleh, Naveed. *The Complete Guide to Article Writing: How to Write Successful Articles for Online and Print Markets*. Ft. Collins, CO: Writer's Digest, 2014.

PERIODICALS

Writer Magazine
25 Braintree Hill Office Park, Suite 404
Braintree, MA 02184
(877) 252-8139
Website: http://www.writermag.com

Writer's Digest
4700 E. Galbraith Road
Cincinnati, OH 45236
(513) 531-2222
Website: http://www.writersdigest.com

WEBSITES

Because of the changing nature of internet links, Rosen Publishing has developed an online list of websites related to the subject of this book. This site is updated regularly. Please use this link to access the list:

http://www.rosenlinks.com/CCWC/writing

CHAPTER 10

SCREENWRITER FOR TELEVISION AND FILM

The feature film and television industries are two of the biggest moneymaking industries in the world, and both require screenwriters. Writers are also needed to create scripts for educational films, promotional films, and newscasts. Working as a screenwriter can be exciting, but it is often a difficult career filled with stumbling blocks. There are a few options for those without a college education, but you must be an undying promoter of your work. Develop skills as a salesperson and grow a thick skin while you're at it.

Screenwriters often work in pairs or groups to bounce ideas around, speak dialogue aloud to make sure it flows, and provide feedback to each other.

WHAT THEY DO

Screenwriting is a demanding career. Once a writer completes a screenplay, he or she needs to sell it. Producers are notoriously demanding, and working with them can be frustrating. Although screenwriters may not need agents to sell their work to smaller production companies, they definitely need agents when dealing with large Hollywood or New York studios.

Script readers want fresh scripts. The writer needs to find a way to breathe new life into old themes. Agents and editors are also looking for colorful characters, highly visual elements that will look spectacular on film, and a hook—an idea that will capture the audience's attention. These elements make screenplays more popular and therefore more profitable.

Some screenwriters begin their careers by writing and producing short films (shorts) or independent films (indies). If you are able to write a short narrative, this is a great way to develop your screenwriting skills and learn the ropes of the filmmaking industry. Some people even create short films and series for streaming online through a site like Funny or Die. Keep in mind, however, that you need to find funding for these two options. This usually means that you will need the help of others who are also hoping to break into the movie-making industry.

Many writers publish their stories or novels before thinking of adapting them into screenplays. Having a novel accepted for publication shows agents and editors that it might make a good film or television script. (Most production companies now prefer to adapt previously written works and use preexisting stories as a way to save money.)

Some experts in the film industry agree that the most important part of a screenplay is the first ten to fifteen pages. This is the information that will either grab readers' attention or cause them to toss your story aside. Once you've grabbed your readers' attention, you need to develop the action of the story. Other experts will tell you that the last ten pages are just as important as the first ten pages. Drawing readers into a closing climax scene

Screenwriter Diablo Cody is the writer of the movies *Juno*, *Young Adulte*, and *Jennifer's Body*, and the TV series *One Mississippi* and *The United States of Tara*.

PITCHING YOUR WORK

The pitch is a vital step for all screenwriters. Pitching a script means selling it verbally to a producer. Pitching your story is more like acting than writing. Here is a list of tips to help you pitch with the best of them.

- Don't just wing it. Some screenwriters are so confident in their speaking abilities that they think the perfect pitch will simply come to them. Many of these people end up losing an opportunity to sell their screenplay because their pitch falls flat. Practice pitching your screenplay to another screenwriter.
- Your pitch should be somewhat detailed but to the point. Aim for a ten-minute plot synopsis.
- Your pitch should focus on a single character. Think of this character as the "star" of your screenplay. Emphasize the traits that will make an actor want to play that character in a movie.
- Unravel the story about the main character. What happens to him or her? What problems does the character face? What are the results of his or her struggle?
- Producers need to know how to market your ideas. Emphasize the genre, or category, of movie that you have written. Point out the type of audience who would want to see it.
- Emphasize the qualities that will make a director want to turn your screenplay into a movie. Directors want a strong story with unique characters.

is as important as wrapping up your ideas without leaving questions unanswered. More than anything the story should feel complete with a beginning, middle, and end.

PREPARING FOR YOUR CAREER

Although watching movies may not seem educational, it will help to improve your storytelling technique. Reading screenplays written by other writers may also help. At the very least, reading screenplays will show you the proper format for a screenplay, without which you simply won't sell your work. It may also help to watch a movie while reading the script at the same time.

You should also try to familiarize yourself with the film and television industry by reading trade magazines, going to film festivals, and participating in screenwriting contests.

JOB OUTLOOK AND SALARY

Earning a salary that provides you with a living wage can take a long time. You may make nothing, especially when working on independent films. Well-known, successful screenwriters can make millions on a single script, in addition to a percentage of what the finished film takes in as profit. Staff screenwriters usually earn an annual salary ranging from $30,000 to $85,000 a year.

SCREENWRITING GLOSSARY

It is important for screenwriters to know how to package their screenplay to best influence those who will be reading it. You will need to know how to create the following types of writing if you expect to sell your screenplay.

LOGLINE One or two sentences at the beginning of a treatment designed to grab the reader's attention. Loglines are also used in face-to-face meetings between writers and producers.

QUERY LETTER As with novelists and magazine writers, screenwriters often sell their screenplays or ideas for screenplays by sending out a well-crafted query letter. The query letter is usually the first contact between a writer and the person or persons who will buy it.

STEP OUTLINE A screenplay summary that includes one sentence for each scene. Some studios expect to see a step outline before accepting a screenplay.

SYNOPSIS A one-page summary of the plot of your screenplay. The synopsis is an important tool when selling your work.

TREATMENT A scene-by-scene summary of the screenplay without dialogue. Treatments are usually about thirty to fifty pages long and include a logline and a one- to three-page synopsis that describes the events and characters. Writers are often paid a portion of their fee upon submitting their treatment.

The screenwriting business is competitive, even more so than careers in book or magazine publishing. It costs far more to make a film than it does to publish a novel. Think of all the people who work on a movie set: actors, directors, writers, camera people, fashion experts, musicians, and many others. Because of their large budgets, movie producers often want to work with established screenwriters who have already written blockbuster screenplays.

This is not to say that screenwriting isn't worth your time or that you cannot succeed at a career in this field. It does mean that you will have to work hard and remain determined, even as the rejection letters pile up. Learn what you can from these rejections and master the rules for preparing and submitting your screenplay as your writing improves. Your chances of selling your script will increase as you build a reputation as a dependable, capable writer. In the meantime, start making your own series and short films to get your name out there. Even a Twitter account with a lot of followers might attract someone to your writing, so be sure to update it regularly.

FOR MORE INFORMATION

ORGANIZATIONS

Writers Guild of America, East
250 Hudson Street, Suite 700
New York, NY 10013
(212) 767-7800
Website: https://www.wgaeast.org
The Writers Guild of America East (WGAE) is a labor
union of thousands of professionals who are the
primary creators of what is seen or heard on television
and film in the United States, as well as the writers of a
growing portion of original digital media content.

Writers Guild of America, West
7000 West 3rd Street
Los Angeles, CA 90048
(323) 951-4000
Website: http://www.wga.org
The Writers Guild is a labor union composed of
the thousands of writers who write the content
for television shows, movies, news programs,
documentaries, animation, internet, and
mobile phones.

BOOKS

Lennon, Thomas, and Robert Ben Garant. *Writing Movies for Fun and Profit: How We Made a Billion Dollars at the Box Office and You Can, Too!* New York, NY: Touchstone, 2012.

On Story: Screenwriters and Filmmakers on Their Iconic Films. Austin, TX: University of Texas Press, 2016.

Trottier, David. *The Screenwriter's Bible: A Complete Guide to Writing, Formatting, and Selling Your Script*. Los Angeles, CA: Silman-James Press, 2014.

WEBSITES

Because of the changing nature of internet links, Rosen Publishing has developed an online list of websites related to the subject of this book. This site is updated regularly. Please use this link to access the list:

http://www.rosenlinks.com/CCWC/writing

CHAPTER 11

COLUMNIST OR OPINION BLOGGER

People who write articles for newspapers and news magazines must stick to the facts. Readers expect an objective and unbiased view of the subject matter, whether it is a local or international news story. However, every writer has his or her own opinion. If you are a writer who yearns to write from a personal point of view and offer your opinions rather than simply reporting the facts, you may want to consider pursuing a career as a columnist or opinion blogger.

WHAT THEY DO

Columnists and bloggers write daily, weekly, or monthly opinion pieces for newspapers, magazines, and online news sites. Political or news columns generally appear in the op-ed pages in a newspaper. Some columnists are even paid to read their column on public radio stations or television news shows. Every columnist writes about something that interests him or her, whether sports, fashion, humor, family life, or cooking. Many write about government and political activities. Others

Columnist Dave Barry won the 1988 Pulitzer Prize for his work. Additionally, he's a bestselling author of multiple books.

write advice columns about personal or motivational topics that follow a specific theme. Still others write humorous pieces about whatever crosses their minds when they sit down at their desks. The one thing all of these columnists have in common is that they are speaking their minds and not just reporting the facts.

Much like newspaper reporters, columnists are curious people who want to know more about many topics. Although columnists use their opinions and personalized writing style to shape their columns, much of their job relies heavily on research.Columnists must be careful to relate the facts of a story, like reporters do, before they express their opinion about it.

Columnists often read the news and listen to current events on both television and radio to come up with ideas and to hear public opinion. The columnist examines the news story or report and then uses his or her personal style to express an opinion about the subject matter. This often makes columns more exciting or interesting than news articles.

COLUMNIST VS. JOURNALIST

Most newspapers and magazines print columns in every issue. But how is a column different from a regular news article? The most important difference is that columns are expressions of the author's opinion and not just a report of the facts. A column is generally shorter than a newspaper or magazine article—usually between four hundred and one thousand words. A column is short enough to read quickly and long enough to entertain its readers with well-developed ideas. It usually has a catchy beginning, a concise but descriptive middle, and a strong ending that readers will remember.

An editorial is another kind of opinion piece. Editorials are generally written by the editorial board of a news organization and appear without bylines. An editorial is usually meant to express the collective opinion of the organization and not that of an individual. Editorials usually take up an entire page of the newspaper, and they are usually about current events. The op-ed page (which is literally opposite the editorial page) features letters to the editor from readers who want to express their own opinions about editorials or other matters.

Some columnists are masters of satire and parody, two writing devices that are never allowed in a news article.

Columnists usually follow a rigid schedule, and they must meet regular deadlines depending on how often the publication for which they write is printed—daily, weekly, monthly, or quarterly. Freelance columnists may get work less frequently, but they must work consistently nonetheless in order to make a solid living. Many freelance columnists become full-time writers for newspapers or magazines after they have built up a significant readership.

As a columnist, you will find that the larger your audience, the more publications will be interested in running your column on a regular basis. Popular columnists often become syndicated. This means that their columns are printed by more than one newspaper. Some columns are printed nationally by as many publications that want to run them. A syndicate is a marketing company that sells your work to as many publications as it can and then takes a portion of the profits earned by those sales. The more publications that print your column, the more money you earn.

PREPARING FOR YOUR CAREER

A good way to start training for a career as a columnist is to write articles for your school newspaper; you might even start your own column. You might also want to start your

Opinion bloggers can work almost anywhere and write about a variety of subjects.

own blog. Joining a debate team will teach you how to effectively express your own opinions about a subject and may offer you some feedback on those opinions.

When training to become a columnist, it is important to read the work of other columnists. Read five or six columnists on a regular basis. Choose the work of a few columnists who write about topics that interest you. Choose a few for other reasons, perhaps simply because they are popular or even because their opinions are different from your own. This will help you become familiar with the basic structure of a column. It will also expose you to different writing styles and ways of thinking, which will help you to establish your own individual style and voice.

JOB OUTLOOK AND SALARY

Some starting columnists can earn between $20,000 and $30,000 a year. More experienced columnists may earn between $60,000 and $100,000 or more. Freelance columnists normally get paid per column, and that amount depends on the individual publication. Syndicates usually take between 40 and 60 percent of the profit.

Most columnists begin their careers as reporters or editors and work their way up to a position as a columnist. Compared to news reporters, there are far fewer positions available for columnists, and former reporters usually secure most of them. Because of this, pursuing a career as a columnist is much easier if you first spend some time as a reporter. It is best to start as a reporter at a newspaper with a small editorial staff. This will allow you the opportunity to move up quickly should a columnist position become available.

FOR MORE INFORMATION

ORGANIZATIONS

The American Society of Journalists and Authors (ASJA)
355 Lexington Avenue, 15th Floor
New York, NY 10017
(212) 997-0947
Website: http://www.asja.org
Founded in 1948, the American Society of Journalists
and Authors is the nation's professional organization
of independent nonfiction writers.

The National Society of Newspaper Columnists (NSNC)
P.O. Box 411532
San Francisco, CA 94141
(415) 488-6762
Website: http://www.columnists.com
The National Society of Newspaper Columnists is a
nonprofit organization that promotes professionalism
and camaraderie among columnists and other writers
of the serial essay, including bloggers.

BOOKS

Avlon, John P., Jesse Angelo, and Errol Louis, eds.
*Deadline Artists: America's Greatest Newspaper
Columns*. New York, NY: The Overlook Press, 2011.

Gutkind, Lee. *You Can't Make This Stuff Up: The Complete Guide to Writing Creative Nonfiction—from Memoir to Literary Journalism and Everything in Between*. Boston, MA: Da Capo Lifelong Books, 2012.

King, Stephen. *On Writing: 10th Anniversary Edition: A Memoir of the Craft*. New York, NY: Scribner, 2010.

Lamott, Anne. B*ird by Bird: Some Instructions on Writing and Life*. New York, NY: Anchor, 1995.

WEBSITES

Because of the changing nature of internet links, Rosen Publishing has developed an online list of websites related to the subject of this book. This site is updated regularly. Please use this link to access the list:

http://www.rosenlinks.com/CCWC/writing

CHAPTER 12

PLAYWRIGHT

Being a playwright has a great deal of historical significance as plays were one of the first forms of entertainment. The ancient Greeks considered playwriting one of the highest forms of art. They wrote plays to teach morals and values and to entertain their audiences. Today, theater productions are vastly popular all over the world, and the theater industry requires a constant influx of scripts written by playwrights of many levels of experience and ability.

WHAT THEY DO

Playwrights write the scripts performed by theater companies. They are sometimes directors or consultants for productions they have written. Playwrights create dramas, comedies, tragedies, mysteries, and musicals. Some break

Plays were one of the first types of entertainment, so being a successful playwright is a highly regarded career.

into the business by selling their work to small town theaters. Major cities have large theater companies.

Overall length categorizes most plays. A one-act play usually lasts no longer than thirty minutes and usually has a single setting. Theaters often show two or more one-act plays in a single evening. Full-length plays run for about an hour or two and include several scene changes. Another type of play that has become popular in recent years (mainly due to playwriting contests) is the ten-minute play. These are plays whose stories unfold and resolve quickly.

Musicals are plays accompanied by music and dancing. The actors may speak some of their lines and sing the others. Some musicals are almost completely performed in song. A team of writers and composers, rather than a single playwright, writes most musicals.

Once you have written a play, you need to find a publisher to print it or a theater company to produce it. Some playwrights prefer to hire agents for this task. As with novels and screenplays, "selling" is a time-consuming process. You can count on rejections, but this is part of the game. Most publishers and theater companies receive far more scripts than they could possibly produce. It is important for you to research the market to find the best possible publisher for your play. For instance, don't send a one-act play to publishing houses that only produce full-length plays. Some publishers require playwrights to send a query letter before remitting an actual play. Some companies accept unsolicited plays. Scripts must be written according to strict guidelines; refer to the directory for more information on manuscript and submission guidelines.

When a publisher accepts a play, it sends the playwright a contract. Once the playwright signs the contract, the publisher publishes an acting copy of the script and advertises it in its catalogue, industry magazines, and online.

SCRIPTS AND SCREENPLAYS

Play scripts are similar to screenplays in form and content, but they are also different in many ways. Playwrights are often considered more literary or artistic in comparison to screenwriters. Screenplays are often action based; plays are often word-based. That is, it is the actual words that engage the audience.

Also, less is usually more when it comes to theater productions. Some of the most successful plays of all time, such as *Death of a Salesman* for example, take place in one single setting. In cases such as these, much of the drama comes from the writing and the performance but also the techniques of makeup artists, fashion designers, set and lighting designers, and special effects people. Keep this in mind when writing a play.

Plays are often much less formulaic than screenplays. As discussed earlier, most film and television producers are looking for film ideas that follow a pattern or a plot that has already been proven to work; that is why sequels are done so frequently. Playwrights, on the other hand, can usually be more inventive with their writing. Theater companies are more interested in a good story than a proven formula. Take, for example, Samuel Beckett's play *Waiting for Godot*, a play about two men waiting for a third man, who in fact never shows up. Very little happens in this play, yet it is one of the most famous plays of all time.

Playwrights usually have much more control over their creations than do screenwriters. Playwrights sometimes make revisions to their scripts even as the play is being rehearsed on stage with actors.

Directors, producers, and theaters browse through these scripts and select the ones they want to show.

PREPARING FOR YOUR CAREER

The best thing to do in order to prep yourself for a career as a playwright is to see as many plays and musicals as possible. You may benefit from playwriting seminars, theater workshops, and writing contests. It would also help to get a job with a theater company. Many theater companies accept volunteer interns for a variety of jobs, from building sets to securing props. Once you are working at a theater company, pay attention behind the scenes and during rehearsals.

JOB OUTLOOK AND SALARY

The pay scale for playwrights varies by the circumstances. Some playwrights receive a set payment for their plays. Many playwrights receive royalties every time a theater performs their play, usually 25 to 50 percent of what the publisher charges. Let's say it costs $50 for a theater to show your play once; $25 goes to you, and $25 goes to the publisher. If the theater shows the play ten times, your royalty check will be $250. Now let's say that ten theaters want to show your play ten times each. Each theater will pay you $250, for a total of $2,500. You also receive a small percentage of the money made for each acting script the publisher sells, often around 10 percent. If the publisher sells fifty scripts at $6 a script, you receive an additional $30. The more plays you have on the market, the more royalty checks you will receive. The more recognizable your name becomes, the longer your plays will run and the more money you will earn.

Playwriting is a competitive profession. Producers have literally thousands of new scripts to choose from in addition to the classics that never go out of style. The good news is that the theater industry is a vastly popular business that is always in need of fresh scripts. Playwrights need to be patient and persistent while they develop their craft. One of the most important things to remember when writing your script is to keep it simple. You may improve your chances of having your play produced if it contains minimal set changes and technical requirements. A play with a smaller scope may be more enticing to producers because it will cost less to produce.

FOR MORE INFORMATION

ORGANIZATIONS

The Playwrights' Center
2301 Franklin Avenue East
Minneapolis, MN 55406
(612) 332-7481
Website: https://pwcenter.org
The Playwrights' Center focuses on both supporting
  playwrights and promoting new plays to production
  at theaters across the country.

Young Playwrights Inc.
PO Box 5134
New York, NY 10185
(212) 594-5440
Website: http://www.youngplaywrights.org
Young Playwrights Inc. is the only professional theater
  in the United States solely dedicated to identifying,
  developing, producing, and promoting playwrights
  aged eighteen and under.

BOOKS

Cole, Toby. *Playwrights on Playwriting: From Ibsen to
  Ionesco*. New York, NY: Cooper Square Press, 2001.

Johann, Susan. *Focus on Playwrights: Portraits and Interviews*. Columbia, SC: University of South Carolina Press, 2016.

Tichler, Rosemarie, and Barry Jay Kaplan. *The Playwright at Work: Conversations*. Evanston, IL: Northwestern University Press, 2012.

WEBSITES

Because of the changing nature of internet links, Rosen Publishing has developed an online list of websites related to the subject of this book. This site is updated regularly. Please use this link to access the list:

http://www.rosenlinks.com/CCWC/writing

CHAPTER 13

ADMINISTRATIVE ASSISTANT

Administrative assistants are in charge of keeping a person or department organized. They take notes and make travel arrangements. Administrative assistants plan meetings, coordinate events, organize files, answer the phone, and write correspondence. Among the many skills an administrative assistant will need, writing is one of the most important.

Administrative assistants write correspondence for a manager, answer the phone, take messages, and handle a variety of unforseen tasks every day as well.

WHAT THEY DO

Administrative assistants "assist" other workers with a wide range of responsibilities. Admins are a vital component to our modern business world. Many businesses and corporations rely on administrative assistants to keep their organizations running smoothly. Without them, many offices would fall apart.

Depending on the company for which they work, administrative assistants may do any or all of the following tasks: answer phones, greet clients and answer their questions, write letters and reports, edit documents, book travel plans, order office supplies, train new employees, set up meetings, take notes, dictate letters, use and maintain office machines, schedule appointments, organize and update records, handle payroll and bookkeeping tasks, and more. In general, administrative assistants make sure the day-to-day activities of an office run smoothly. In doing their job, administrative assistants allow supervisors, managers, and other employees to perform their own jobs more efficiently.

Some admin positions require specialized skills. For example, an administrative assistant who works for a real estate office must know how to close a sale on a house and must understand the jargon and paperwork specific to the real estate business. Legal admins must know how to take specific information from clients and are often the people who interview clients before an attorney is even called in to review a case.

Administrative assistants are usually under pressure to perform quickly and efficiently. Some work for several managers or supervisors, while others work for just one. Some may be expected to work long hours or to travel frequently. Whatever their situation, administrative assistants need to be cooperative, organized, and dependable. They need to be able to fulfill a request quickly without asking how to get it done. Administrative assistants are often thought of as problem solvers. When the photocopier breaks down, for instance, the adept admin knows how to get it working again. If they cannot fix the problem themselves, they quickly contact a person who can fix the problem. This type of reaction to office problems allows supervisors and managers to continue working with as little interruption as possible.

People skills are very important for administrative assistants. They must be able to communicate clearly and professionally, in person and on the telephone. Individuals who get nervous when talking to clients and supervisors may not make it very long as an administrative assistant, regardless of how well they perform their daily tasks.

There are many kinds of writing in which an administrative assistant must be proficient. Writing an effective business letters is only one facet of the job. An admin must also write reports, invoices, memos, schedules, notes, and much more. Administrative assistants must have effective writing skills, be proficient at many types of software, and be able to write any of the aforementioned documents at a moment's notice.

PREPARING FOR YOUR CAREER

High school instruction in math, English, and business will prepare you for a job as an administrative assistant. Most employers will expect their administrative assistants to be familiar with computers and standard business software. Administrative assistants need efficient typing skills (at least sixty words per minute) and may also need to know shorthand

Administrative assistants need to be competent in computer use and the latest software in order to handle tasks quickly and efficiently.

for dictating important information in a hurry. Having a working knowledge of these topics will surely give you a leg up on other job applicants.

Many administrative assistants take classes and receive certification as a professional admin, which increases their chances of finding a job that pays well. You can learn more about through the association in the directory that follows this chapter.

JOB OUTLOOK AND SALARY

Salaries for administrative assistants depend on several factors, including the employer, the type of business, and the

INTERVIEW WITH AN ADMINISTRATIVE ASSISTANT

Amanda Smith has been an administrative assistant for a construction company for two years. She has also worked as an administrative assistant for a multimillion-dollar telecommunications company and as a medical office assistant.

WHAT DO YOU LIKE BEST ABOUT YOUR JOB?
I enjoy dealing with many different people, from the common homeowner to savvy businessmen and businesswomen. Also,

knowing that I helped someone feel more comfortable and happier with their new surroundings, whether it is their home, office, cottage, garage, or deck, is a great feeling.

WHAT DO YOU LIKE LEAST ABOUT YOUR JOB?

Some people that I deal with are not very friendly. There are a lot of people out there who will try to get out of paying for things. I believe that you get what you pay for. If you want quality work there is a price. That is why it is so important that a contract is drawn up to protect the contractor, the homeowner, or the business owner.

WHAT ADVICE WOULD YOU GIVE TO SOMEONE WHO WAS THINKING ABOUT PURSING A CAREER AS AN ADMINSTRATIVE ASSISTANT?

Make sure that you are a people person, someone who likes to interact with all kinds of people. Strive to be an efficient self-motivator. Try not to loose your cool. Always remember that you have to be held accountable for your actions or things you might say in anger.

HOW IS WRITING IMPORTANT TO YOUR JOB?

I need to write the invoices that are received by our customers. I generate monthly reports for our accountant that must be precise and worded professionally. I create spreadsheets for the materials we buy and use on jobs. Each week I need to document the work hours for each employee and appoint his or her time to the correct job for invoicing. I also have to document the money coming in and going out, including the payroll and monthly bills.

level of experience. Administrative assistants earn an average of $36,500 a year. Experienced administrative assistants may earn a salary of up to $60,000 a year. In general, any admin experience that you have will increase your annual salary.

The outlook for admin careers is very good. In fact, it is one of the quickest growing occupations in America. Think of all the businesses in your town or city that depend on administrative assistants to keep things running smoothly. There are plenty of admin jobs to go around, but it is the most conscientious and skillful administrative assistants who meet with the greatest success. Some administrative assistants are promoted to managerial position once they have been with a company long enough and understand how it works.

FOR MORE INFORMATION

ORGANIZATIONS

International Association of Administrative Professionals
(IAAP)
10502 NW Ambassador Drive
P.O. Box 20404
Kansas City, MO 64195-0404
(816) 891-6600
Website: http://www.iaap-hq.org
IAAP is a not-for-profit professional association for
administrative professionals.

BOOKS

Stroman, James, Kevin Wilson, and Jennifer Wauson.
Administrative Assistant's and Secretary's Handbook.
New York, NY: AMACOM, 2014.

WEBSITES

Because of the changing nature of internet links, Rosen
Publishing has developed an online list of websites
related to the subject of this book. This site is updated
regularly. Please use this link to access the list:

http://www.rosenlinks.com/CCWC/writing

CHAPTER 14

FACT CHECKER

Do you remember seemingly irrelevant facts and figures? Do you have a photographic memory? Besides becoming a regular contestant on the game show *Jeopardy*, you might want to think about a career as a fact checker. A fact checker is a valuable addition to any editorial staff. Fact checkers are often the first line of defense when it comes to identifying incorrect statistics, name spellings, dates, information surrounding historical events, and up-to-date contact information. Fact checkers often assist editors and copy editors so that they can better accomplish their jobs with speed and accuracy.

WHAT THEY DO

The words that we read in the newspaper are not always accurate. The Pulitzer Prize–winning writer and columnist Ellen Goodman once wrote, "In journalism, there has always been a tension between getting it first and getting it right." Some news reporters and journalists get caught up in the race to be first that they forget (or simply neglect) to be right. Writers, editors, copy editors, and proofreaders all help to create factual news stories and articles; fact checkers base their entire careers on getting accurate information.

Fact checkers have a lot of responsibility. It is their duty to help the publication for which they work to avoid litigation resulting from printing incorrect or biased information. At the same time, fact checkers often need to work swiftly, leaving little time to double check articles or manuscripts for accuracy. Most publications take pride in providing information. Retractions are a great source of embarrassment for any newspaper, magazine, or publishing house.

Fact checkers constantly learn new information and build upon previous knowledge. Fact checkers learn as they work and even get a thrill from solving problems. Books of all kinds are very important to the fact checker's job, from dictionaries and encyclopedias, to more specialized resources, such as medical books and art history texts. Other forms of information that fact checkers use on a daily basis include online sources, telephone contacts, and alliances with writers and editors. Fact checkers quickly build a large collection of resources that they can consult at a moment's notice.

Fact checkers need to keep an open mind. Although a fact checker might be very experienced and knowledgeable in many areas, there are always instances when they must investigate a field in which they are unfamiliar. Fact checkers must work with writers, editors, copy editors, designers, and others when preparing text for publication. It only makes the process more difficult when one of those workers refuses to accept input from the others. Regardless of how good a fact checker is, he or she should always be open to suggestions from other members of the editorial staff. A good fact checker also knows when to seek the help of others.

Despite having a large team of editors, proofreaders, and fact checkers, mistakes still manage to slip through the cracks. Criticism for these errors often falls on the fact checkers. Don't get upset about criticism. Instead, investigate the errors and learn the truth.

PREPARING FOR YOUR CAREER

Fact checkers must have a firm grasp on the English language. It also helps to read as much as you can. Knowledge—any kind of knowledge—will help you to save time since you will spend less time searching for information.

A good way to train for a career as a fact checker is to scan the daily newspaper for errors every day. Researching facts and finding mistakes will give you a taste of what it is like to be a professional fact checker.

JOB OUTLOOK AND SALARY

Beginning fact checkers may make about $25,000 to $30,000 a year. They make more with experience and even more if they are promoted to higher positions in the company. Freelancers usually make between $20 and $30 an hour, or sometimes more, depending on the content of the publication. Most fact-checking jobs are held by freelancers, so it's important to cast a wide net when pursuing a career in the field.

Becoming a fact checker is often a starting point in a person's editorial career. You may move from fact checker to copy editor, editor, or reporter, and then on to a position

Magazines like *Time* employ fact checkers. A big factual error can lead to reduced sales and questions about a magazine's journalistic integrity.

as managing or senior editor. Others have long careers as fact checkers.

In general, any company that prints nonfiction might benefit from an on-staff fact checker. Depending on the size of the publication, fact checking may be the responsibility of editors, copy editors, and/or proofreaders. Daily newspapers do not hire fact checkers because there simply is no time for them to do their job. Newspapers often expect their reporters and editors to check facts. Weekly news magazines like *Time* are more likely to hire fact checkers.

Many fact checkers make excellent money as freelancers. Some specialize in a certain areas of publishing, such as high school science textbooks. Some will tackle a variety of material, especially if the price is right. Many publishers prefer to use freelance fact checkers because it is cheaper to hire them as they are needed, rather than pay a full-time employee.

Fact checkers need a wide range of resources to do their jobs well. Years ago, fact checkers spent long hours between dusty library stacks. Today—thanks to the Internet—fact checkers have reference materials at their fingertips at all times.

FOR MORE INFORMATION

ORGANIZATIONS

FactCheck.org
Annenberg Public Policy Center
202 S. 36th Street
Philadelphia, PA 19104
(215) 898-9400
Website: http://www.factcheck.org
FactCheck.org monitors the factual accuracy of what
is said by major US political players in the form of TV
ads, debates, speeches, interviews, and news releases.

BOOKS

Smith, Sarah Harrison. *The Fact Checker's Bible: A Guide to Getting It Right*. New York, NY: Anchor, 2004.

WEBSITES

Because of the changing nature of internet links, Rosen Publishing has developed an online list of websites related to the subject of this book. This site is updated regularly. Please use this link to access the list:

http://www.rosenlinks.com/CCWC/writing

CHAPTER 15

COPYWRITER

Just think of how many advertisements you encounter on a daily basis: travel brochures, billboards, flyers, catalogues, radio and television commercials, online ads, infomercials, and even coupons and ads in newspapers. The abundance of advertisements shows how important copywriters are to companies and businesses. Effective copywriters are needed to sell just about everything, from candy bars to luxury cars.

Copywriters are responsible for every line of text you see in advertisements. They must create thoughtful, humorous, and smart text that sells.

WHAT THEY DO

Copywriters write all of the copy that's used in advertising. They write ad copy (the words that make up written or spoken advertisements) for all forms of media. Some copywriters write for public relations firms, marketing campaigns, or trade magazines. Freelance copywriters must be versatile enough to write copy for a wide range of products and purposes. Experienced copywriters often work for advertising agencies. In fact, the majority of advertisement work today is handled by advertising agencies.

While good writing skills are essential for copywriters, they must also be able to study a product and highlight its strongest selling points. In order to create effective copy, copywriters must research the product, the company selling it, and the people who will buy it. Much of this information often comes directly from the company the copywriter works for, but it never hurts to back up this source of information with independent research.

In general, a good copywriter must be observant, persuasive, and thoughtful. Copywriters must be able to work quickly and efficiently, and they are often under pressure to finish an assignment. Once a copywriter receives an assignment, he or she often has very little time to write engaging copy. Many copywriters receive multiple assignments. Not only does this make deadlines more challenging, it also forces a copywriter to quickly switch from one assignment to another. A copywriter may be required to write about disposable razors one minute and frozen vegetables the next.

Deadlines are crucial. Companies expect timely results when they hire a person or a business to write its copy. Newspapers are printed every day. Magazines usually come out once a month. Television and radio ads run constantly. This continuous flow of advertisements is created nonstop by thousands of talented writers.

AD AGENCIES

Advertising agencies are independent companies that bring a fresh perspective to their clients' products and services. An ad agency can be very small—as few as one or two people—or they can include hundreds of workers and many divisions. Some specialize in a particular kind of advertising, such as television commercials or internet advertising.

Advertising agencies employ copywriters to write the text that will be used in their clients' advertisements. They may write the copy used for television commercials, radio spots, print advertisements, packaging, billboards, brochures, and so on. Sometimes they are assigned multiple projects at the same time. Copywriters working for agencies may also be required to create a central theme that will be used in a series of commercials for the same product or company, creating copy that will be easily recognizable by consumers for extended periods.

Copywriters are creative writers. When it comes down to it, however, copywriters must be experts in persuasive writing. It is their job to convince the audience that they want the product that is being marketed. Copywriters know what people want from a product. They use this knowledge to focus their writing. Copywriters are adept at grabbing the attention of readers, viewers, and listeners with a variety of techniques. They write memorable slogans and catchy head-lines. They know when to appeal to their audience's practical side and when to appeal to their emotional side.

PREPARING FOR YOUR CAREER

Many businesses and advertising firms expect copywriters to have a college degree, but this is not the case with all of them. Many businesses will hire assistant copywriters who do not have a degree. This is an excellent opportunity for you to get your foot in the door and start learning the ropes from copywriters with experience.

Most employers, however, will expect you to have some writing experience. Advertising agencies usually hire individuals with three to five years experience as a copywriter, so you may have to work your way up to this position.

Copywriters who create copy for print media may also want to familiarize themselves with standard graphic arts techniques and computer programs. This will help them to better visualize the finished product as they write. It will also make it easier for them to work hand-in-hand with the graphic artists who will be transforming their words into visual advertisements. Copywriters will also want to create an online portfolio that can easily be shared with potential employers and clients.

JOB OUTLOOK AND SALARY

Copywriter salaries may start at about $31,000 to $50,000 a year or more. Once you work your way up to copywriter, however, you can make between $60,000 and $80,000, perhaps more depending on the company and your experience. The most successful copywriters can make a six-figure income, but this takes years of experience.

Copywriting and advertising jobs are plentiful in our market-oriented society. However, this does not mean that becoming a copywriter is an easy task. The job market can be fierce, and copywriters need both experience and confidence to succeed. Plan to start out on the low end of the pay scale. Many copywriters begin this way, and many also succeed. Be observant, persistent, and confident in your abilities.

FOR MORE INFORMATION

ORGANIZATIONS

American Marketing Association
130 E. Randolph Street
Chicago, IL 60601
(800) 262-1150
Website: http://www.marketingpower.com
The American Marketing Association provides ways for
marketers and academics to connect with the people
and resources they need to be successful.

BOOKS

Bly, Robert W. *The Copywriter's Handbook: A Step-By-Step
Guide to Writing Copy That Sells*. New York, NY: Holt, 2006.

WEBSITES

Because of the changing nature of internet links, Rosen
Publishing has developed an online list of websites
related to the subject of this book. This site is updated
regularly. Please use this link to access the list:

http://www.rosenlinks.com/CCWC/writing

GLOSSARY

ADMINISTRATIVE Relating to the management of business matters.

AGENT An expert in a field, such as book publishing, who acts on behalf of a client; a business representative.

DICTATE To speak or read to a person so he or she can record the words in writing.

FREELANCE To pursue a career without working for any one company or publication.

GRAPHIC DESIGN The art or profession of using design elements (such as pictures and text) to convey meaning.

PERIODICAL A publication printed with a fixed interval of time between issues.

PROOF A sheet of paper covered with text that is meant to be compared to an earlier form with the purpose of finding and marking errors.

QUERY LETTER A formal letter meant to introduce a writer and his or her work to an agent, editor, or publisher.

ROYALTIES Money paid to the creator of a work of art for the use of that work of art.

SCRUTINIZE To examine closely.

STYLE GUIDE A book detailing a standard way of writing.

SYNDICATE A group of publications that share news stories and/or articles.

BIBLIOGRAPHY

Business Insider. "22 Lessons from Stephen King on How to Be a Great Writer." August 11, 2015. http://www.businessinsider.com/stephen-king-on-how-to-write-2014-8/#1-stop-watching-television-instead-read-as-much-as-possible-1.

Goudreau, Jenna. "Top 10 Tips for Young Aspiring Journalists." *Forbes*, November 9, 2012. http://www.forbes.com/sites/jennagoudreau/2012/11/09/top-10-tips-for-young-aspiring-journalists/#1d812c4338df.

Hurd, Rebecca Smith. "Get Paid to Be a Word Nerd." Writer's Digest, May 17, 2011. http://www.writersdigest.com/writing-articles/by-writing-goal/get-published-sell-my-work/get-paid-to-be-a-word-nerd.

Strachan, Derryck. "10 Top Tips for Being a Successful Copywriter." *Guardian*, December 5, 2013. https://www.theguardian.com/careers/become-a-copywriter-top-tips.

INDEX

ABOUT THE AUTHOR

Rebecca Pelos is a nonfiction writer with experience in job hunting and career guidance. She lives in Tennessee.

Greg Roza has written several books for Rosen Publishing. He lives in New York City.

PHOTO CREDITS

Cover, p. 1 mimagephotography/Shutterstock.com; pp. 4–5 LOFTFLOW/Shutterstock.com; p. 9 Universal History Archive/Universal Images Group/Getty Images; p. 14 © iStockphoto.com/mihailomilovanovic; p. 23 © iStockphoto.com/nicoletaionescu; p. 25 aerogondo2/Shutterstock.com; p. 36 © iStockphoto.com/vm; p. 39 Pixsooz/Shutterstock.com; p. 45 Chip Somodevilla/Getty Images; p. 49 Erika Cross/Shutterstock.com; p. 56 © iStockphoto.com/Rawpixel Ltd; p. 64 Andrey_Popov/Shutterstock.com; p. 70 Niloo/Shutterstock.com; p. 73 Rawpixel.com/Shutterstock.com; pp. 78–79 © iStockphoto.com/Nicolas McComber; p. 81 Bryan Chan/Los Angeles Times/Getty Images; p. 89 Jason Connel/Getty Images; p. 92 ESB Professional/Shutterstock.com; p. 97 criben/Shutterstock.com; p. 104 Monkey Business Images/Shutterstock.com; p. 107 Undrey/Shutterstock.com; p. 115 Chris Hondros/Getty Images; p. 118 f11photo/Shutterstock.com; cover and interior design elements © iStockphoto.com/David Shultz (dots), Melamory/Shutterstock.com (hexagon pattern), Lost & Taken (boxed text background texture), bioraven/Shutterstock.com (chapter opener pages icons).

Designer: Brian Garvey; Editor and Photo Researcher: Bethany Bryan